The ATTACK ON PEARL HARBOR

A DAY THAT CHANGED AMERICA

by Christy Serrano

CAPSTONE PRESS
a capstone imprint

Capstone Captivate is published by Capstone Press, an imprint of Capstone.
1710 Roe Crest Drive, North Mankato, Minnesota 56003
www.capstonepub.com

Library of Congress Cataloging-in-Publication Data
Names: Serrano, Christy, author.
Title: The attack on Pearl Harbor : a day that changed America / by Christy Serrano.
Description: North Mankato : Capstone Press, an imprint of Capstone, [2022] | Includes bibliographical references and index. | Audience: Ages 8-11 | Audience: Grades 4-6 | Summary: "On December 7, 1941, Japan's surprise attack on the U.S. naval base in Pearl Harbor, Hawaii, propelled the United States into World War II. Now readers can step back in time to learn what led up to the attack, how the tragic event unfolded, and the ways in which one infamous day changed America forever"-- Provided by publisher.
Identifiers: LCCN 2021012678 (print) | LCCN 2021012679 (ebook) | ISBN 9781663920799 (paperback) | ISBN 9781663905833 (hardcover) | ISBN 9781663905802 (pdf) | ISBN 9781663905826 (Kindle edition)
Subjects: LCSH: Pearl Harbor (Hawaii), Attack on, 1941--Juvenile literature. | World War, 1939-1945--Causes--Juvenile literature.
Classification: LCC D767.92 .S387 2022 (print) | LCC D767.92 (ebook) | DDC 940.54/26693--dc23
LC record available at https://lccn.loc.gov/2021012678
LC ebook record available at https://lccn.loc.gov/2021012679

Summary: On December 7, 1941, Japan's surprise attack on the U.S. naval base in Pearl Harbor, Hawaii, drove the United States into World War II. Step back in time to learn what led up to the attack, how the tragic event unfolded, and the ways in which one infamous day changed America forever.

Image Credits
Alamy: 508 collection, 11; Bridgeman Images: © Look and Learn, 4; DVIC: NARA, 13, 25, 27; Getty Images: New York Times Co., 23, The LIFE Picture Collection/Life Magazine/Ralph Morse, 22; Library of Congress: 6; Newscom: Everett Collection, 20, Pictures From History, 9; Shutterstock: Alexander Oganezov, 21, Atoly (design element), cover and throughout, Chase Nutfield, 7; U.S. National Archives: 26; U.S. Naval History and Heritage Command: 5, U.S. National Archives, 17, U.S. National Archives/U.S. Army Signal Corps Collection, cover, 18, U.S. National Archives/U.S. Navy, 8, 10, 12, 14, 15, 19, 24; XNR Productions: 16

Editorial Credits
Editor: Eric Braun; Designer: Heidi Thompson; Media Researcher: Svetlana Zhurkin; Production Specialist: Laura Manthe

Consultant Credits
Colonel Dennis P. Mroczkowski, U.S. Marine Corps Reserve

All internet sites appearing in back matter were available and accurate when this book was sent to press.

TABLE OF CONTENTS

Words in **bold** are in the glossary.

INTRODUCTION

It was early on December 7, 1941. The roar of airplane engines cracked the quiet morning. A thick wave of Japanese fighter planes and bombers packed the sky over Hawaii. They flew very low. Witnesses said they could almost see the faces of the pilots.

Japan had been fighting a war in Asia. It was looking to expand its **empire** into the Pacific Ocean. The United States had wanted to stay out of wars in Asia and Europe. Still, Japan believed the U.S. was a threat. They launched this surprise attack on Pearl Harbor. They hoped to weaken the U.S. naval **fleet** there.

The Sunday morning of December 7, 1941, was violently interrupted as Japan attacked Pearl Harbor.

Smoke filled the air as the USS *Shaw* exploded after being bombed.

Japanese planes dropped bombs and **torpedoes**. They destroyed or damaged ships and aircraft. That day, 2,403 Americans were killed. Another 1,178 were wounded. The attack brought the U.S. into World War II.

5

CHAPTER 1

ROAD TO WAR

Americans had been following news about the wars in Europe and Asia. Germany's dictator, Adolph Hitler, **invaded** Poland in 1939. Then, Germany took over other countries in Europe. These included France, Belgium, and the Netherlands. Italy worked with the German army. Their **alliance** was known as the Axis. Japan joined the Axis in 1940.

In September 1939, German troops made their way to Poland's capital, Warsaw.

Many countries fought back against the Axis. They were known as the Allies. They included Great Britain, France, and the Soviet Union.

Most Americans still remembered World War I. It lasted from 1914 to 1918. Over 100,000 Americans lost their lives. More than 40 million people were killed or wounded worldwide. As Hitler moved his armies across Europe, another world war became certain. Americans did not want to join another war.

FACT

People called World War I "the war to end all wars." It was so terrible that it was hard to imagine anyone would ever want to go to war again.

More than 4,000 American soldiers killed in World War I are buried at St. Mihiel American Cemetery and Memorial in France.

Growing Threat in the Pacific

In 1931, Japan invaded China. Japan wanted to expand its empire in Asia. War broke out between the countries in 1937. President Roosevelt was alarmed. He moved the U.S. Pacific Fleet of 130 vessels to the naval base at Pearl Harbor. Pearl Harbor is on the island of Oahu, Hawaii. It was closer to Asia. Roosevelt hoped the move would discourage Japan from taking over more Asian countries.

Pearl Harbor naval base

Japan continued its takeover in 1940 by moving into an area that today includes the countries Vietnam, Laos, and Cambodia.

In 1940, Japan marched into a part of southeast Asia. President Roosevelt responded by ending sales of oil to Japan. This move was meant to hurt Japan's military. It needed the oil for its military forces.

Japan talked with the U.S. about restarting oil sales. But meanwhile, it planned to attack Pearl Harbor. Japan wanted to weaken the U.S. Pacific Fleet. That would give Japan time to occupy other countries in Asia and the Pacific Ocean. The U.S. would not be able to stop it.

As the Japanese military prepared for its strike, military members gathered information on the Pearl Harbor naval base and drew detailed maps.

In November 1941, submarines, aircraft carriers, and other vessels secretly left Japan. They headed toward Pearl Harbor. They kept radio silence as they moved. They took a different path across the Pacific Ocean. This helped Japan keep the plan a secret. On December 2, the Japanese fleet drew close to Hawaii. Japan's ships were darkened. American planes or ships would not be able to see them.

A Japanese aircraft carrier heading toward Hawaii for the surprise attack

CHAPTER 2

SURPRISE ATTACK

Before dawn on December 7, Japan's carriers were about 230 miles (370 kilometers) away from Hawaii. Planes took off from the carriers. They flew toward the harbor. American radar operators noticed a large number of planes coming. They told an army officer. But he said to ignore it. He thought the planes were American bombers. The bombers were scheduled to arrive that day.

Japanese aircraft preparing to take off from a carrier on the morning of December 7, 1941

First Wave of Attacks

The planes were not American bombers. It was the first wave of attack planes. The Americans were completely unprepared. Their ships were anchored to the docks. The airplanes were parked on the airfields. It would not be easy to move equipment to fight back.

Nearly 200 Japanese planes approached the harbor. Japanese Captain Mitsuo Fuchida sent the message "Tora! Tora! Tora!" to the fleet. In English, it means "Tiger! Tiger! Tiger!" It was a code that meant the Americans were going to be surprised.

Smoke started to rise from an airfield as Japan began its attack.

The first wave of Japanese planes arrived at the harbor at 7:55 a.m. They rained bombs on the U.S. Pacific Fleet. American sailors on the battleships ran up to their decks. They fired **anti-aircraft** guns at the enemy planes. Bomb explosions caused fires on the ships. Thick clouds of smoke filled the sky. This made it hard for the sailors to see the planes flying above their ships.

The USS *Shaw* burned after Japanese dive-bombing attacks.

Nearby airfields were also targeted so American pilots could not take off to fight back.

FACT

By the end of the first wave, all of the battleships in the harbor had either sunk or been damaged.

At the same time, another group of Japanese **dive bombers** flew to nearby airfields. They attacked American planes.

Second Wave of Attacks

At 8:50 a.m., about 170 more Japanese planes arrived. It was the second wave of attack. The planes dropped more bombs. Sailors on ships that were not destroyed fought back with anti-aircraft guns. The survivors of one ship swam through blazing oil on the water. They climbed aboard other ships to fire back. A junior officer took a motorboat across the harbor. He drove through a hail of enemy machine-gun fire. He saved almost 100 men from a sinking battleship.

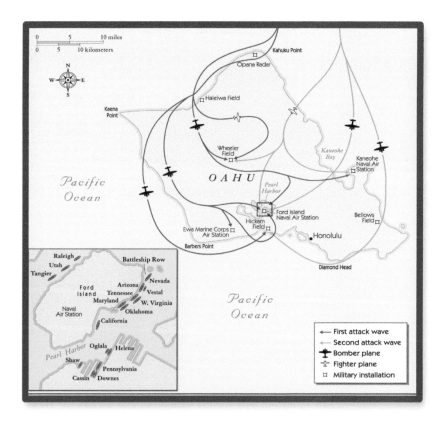

The two waves of attack on Pearl Harbor

The USS *Solace* was one of the few ships not damaged during bombing, and its crew worked to save the wounded.

While many Americans fought, others helped those who were hurt. The USS *Solace* was a hospital ship. Its crew included doctors, nurses, and **corpsmen**. Teams from the USS *Solace* traveled on motorboats to burning ships. They rescued wounded sailors and brought them back to the *Solace* to be treated.

The USS *West Virginia* was one of several ships sunk in the bombing.

By 9:45 a.m., all enemy planes were gone. Yet the U.S. Pacific Fleet continued to burn. Thick, oily smoke hung in the air. More than 15 of the 100 ships at Pearl Harbor were sunk, damaged, or destroyed. This included seven of the eight battleships that were also targeted by Japanese bombers. One hundred eighty-eight planes were destroyed. Thousands of Americans were killed or wounded.

USS *NEVADA*

The battleship USS *Nevada* tried to escape from the harbor. But Japanese dive bombers chased it. They dropped one torpedo and many bombs. The damaged ship fought back, firing at enemy planes. But it began to sink. It was ordered to stop its escape and run onto the beach. That way, it would not block the narrow entryway to the harbor.

Although heavily damaged at Pearl Harbor, the USS *Nevada* would later return to action in 1943.

19

CHAPTER 3

AMERICA REACTS

Soon after the attack, President Roosevelt let Americans know that the country had been attacked. He used newspaper and radio bulletins to spread the news quickly. Millions of Americans were listening to radio broadcasts of football games or comedy shows. Then the news broke. They were asked to stay calm and listen for updates.

President Roosevelt first spoke directly to the nation over radio two days after the surprise Pearl Harbor attack.

Morning newspapers had already been published before the attack. So publishers released "extra" newspaper editions. Many had headlines that read: "WAR! OAHU BOMBED BY JAPANESE PLANES."

Americans had been aware of the bad relationship with Japan. But they were shocked by the attack on Pearl Harbor. Their shock soon turned to outrage.

The *Honolulu Star-Bulletin* first extra edition

People who lived in Honolulu worried about another attack by air. They also feared enemy troops landing on the islands to invade their neighborhoods. The city was placed under **martial law**. This meant the military controlled life in the towns and cities. They would be ready in case of an attack. People covered their windows with black paper or cloth. They turned off lights in the evening. This would help stop bombers from finding cities.

Honolulu and other cities held blackouts, where lights were turned off or hidden, to guard against another enemy attack.

BOY AND GIRL SCOUTS PITCH IN

Many people helped with the recovery in Honolulu, including the Boy and Girl Scouts. They worked at first aid stations. They helped to black out windows. They rode their bicycles to deliver urgent messages to individuals and places such as fire stations, businesses, and factories.

Delivering messages was one way Boy Scouts helped their communities during the war.

CHAPTER 4

AMERICA GOES TO WAR

The day after the attack, President Roosevelt gave a speech to Congress. It was broadcast to the nation over radio. He said that December 7, 1941, was a date that would "live in **infamy**." People would always remember it as a terrible day.

Congress voted to declare war on Japan. Many Americans were eager to help their country fight back. They rushed to recruiting stations. World War I veterans, high school graduates, and others volunteered for the military.

Americans across the nation, even sailors out at sea, tuned into the president's speech in which he asked Congress to declare war on Japan.

Japanese-American Internment

There was a dark side to the U.S. response to war. The U.S. government unfairly believed that Japanese Americans could not be trusted. On February 19, 1942, President Roosevelt ordered Japanese Americans to be separated from the rest of society.

About 120,000 Japanese Americans were forced to live in **internment** camps. They were allowed to bring only clothing and basic supplies. They had to wait until after the end of 1945 before the U.S. government would allow them to leave and return to their lives.

In April 1942, people of Japanese descent arrived at Santa Anita Assembly Center, a camp in California that had once been a racetrack.

25

End of War

The Japanese attack on Pearl Harbor changed the course of history. It pushed the U.S. into World War II. The U.S. military joined the Allies fighting against Axis forces in the Pacific and Europe.

FACT

The United States observes National Pearl Harbor Remembrance Day every December 7. Americans remember and honor those who died in the attack.

A poster calling on Americans to get payback for the Pearl Harbor attack

AVENGE PEARL HARBOR

OUR BULLETS WILL DO IT

On September 2, 1945, World War II came to an official end as U.S. General Douglas MacArthur (seated) and Japanese officials signed the surrender papers.

The war lasted four more years. Hitler killed millions of Jewish people and others. This mass killing became known as the Holocaust. The Allies finally brought an end to the fighting in August 1945 after the U.S. dropped atomic bombs on two Japanese cities. One bomb was dropped on Hiroshima, and a second bomb was dropped on Nagasaki. Japan surrendered after the bombings, and the war ended. The Allies freed the countries the Axis had taken over. But by then, about 75 million people had died in the war.

The U.S. had hoped to avoid war. But after the terrible attack on Pearl Harbor, it saw no other choice but to join the Allies.

TIMELINE

JULY 7, 1937: Japan invades China.

SEPTEMBER 1, 1939: Germany invades Poland, which leads to the outbreak of World War II.

SPRING 1940: Roosevelt moves the fleet to Pearl Harbor.

NOVEMBER 26, 1941: Japan's fleet leaves for Pearl Harbor.

DECEMBER 7, 1941:

7:02 A.M.: A large number of unidentified aircraft are detected on radar. Army privates report this to their lieutenant.

7:20 A.M.: An army lieutenant tells the privates to ignore it. He thinks the aircraft are the U.S. bombers scheduled to arrive that morning.

7:53 A.M.: Japanese Captain Mitsuo Fuchida sends a signal, "Tora! Tora! Tora!"

7:55 A.M.: The first wave of the Japanese air attack on Pearl Harbor and the airfields begins.

8:10 A.M.: The USS *Arizona* explodes when an armor-piercing bomb hits an ammunition magazine. More than 1,100 sailors die aboard the ship.

8:40 A.M.: The USS *Nevada* makes its way down the channel toward open water.

8:50 A.M.: The second wave of the Japanese air attack begins.

9:45 A.M.: Japanese planes head back to their aircraft carriers. The attack is over.

DECEMBER 8, 1941: The U.S. officially declares war on the Empire of Japan.

DECEMBER 11, 1941: Germany and Italy declare war on the U.S., bringing the nation into the war against the entire Axis forces.

MAY 7, 1945: The war in Europe ends with Germany's surrender.

AUGUST 6, 1945: An atomic bomb is dropped on the Japanese city of Hiroshima.

AUGUST 9, 1945: An atomic bomb is dropped on the Japanese city of Nagasaki.

AUGUST 14, 1945: The war in Asia ends with Japan's surrender.

GLOSSARY

alliance (uh-LY-uhnts)—an agreement between groups to work together

anti-aircraft (an-ty-AYRE-craft)—describes weapons designed to defend against attacks from the air

corpsman (KORZ-man)—an enlisted member of a military medical unit

dive bomber (DIVE BAH-muhr)—a military plane that releases bombs while doing a steep dive toward the target

empire (EM-pire)—a large territory ruled by a powerful leader

fleet (FLEET)—a group of ships under a single command

infamy (IN-fuh-mee)—the state of being well-known for something bad

internment (IN-turn-mehnt)—the placement of an enemy or suspicious person under guard

invade (in-VADE)—to send armed forces into another country in order to take it over

martial law (MAR-shuhl LAW)—the control of a people by the government's military, instead of by civilian forces, often during an emergency

torpedo (tor-PEE-doh)—an underwater missile designed to explode when it hits a target

READ MORE

Fowler, Natalie. *A Pearl Harbor Time Capsule: Artifacts of the Surprise Attack on the U.S.* North Mankato, MN: Capstone, 2021.

Williams, Brian. *World War II.* New York: DK Children, 2017.

Zullo, Allan. *Heroes of Pearl Harbor.* New York: Scholastic, 2016.

INTERNET SITES

Britannica Kids: Pearl Harbor
kids.britannica.com/students/article/Pearl-Harbor/276327

DK findout!: Pearl Harbor
dkfindout.com/uk/history/world-war-ii/pearl-harbor/

Ducksters: World War II: Attack on Pearl Harbor
ducksters.com/history/world_war_ii/pearl_harbor_attack.php

INDEX